In Mud Season

Marcia Rajnus Goldberg

CHAPBOOKS BY MARCIA RAJNUS GOLDBERG

Still in Song, Poets' Mimeo Cooperative, Burlington, Vermont, October 1976.

Waking/Seasons (with Judith Yarnall), Poets' Mimeo Cooperative, 1978.

Kill Devil.Hills (illustrated by Artie Gold). Poets Mimeo Cooperative, Charlotte, Vermont, 1979.

Hot Teas, Spotswood Press, Montreal, 1986.

In
Mud
Season

MARCIA RAJNUS GOLDBERG

eɱpуƦeⱥⱢ
P R E S S

In Mud Season © 1999 by Marcia Rajnus Goldberg

EMPYREAL PRESS
P.O. Box 1746 Place du Parc
Montreal Quebec Canada H2W 2R7

Cover by Beatrice Urich
"Umbrellas" Medium: Photo-Collage
Book designed & typeset in Sabon by Sasigraphix.
Printed in Canada by AGMV Marquis.

"Camel's Hump" appeared in *The Stowe School Sampler;* "Cetus, Unfolding", "Delilah/Sheherazade", "Sucker", "Winter Home", "Nice Girl", appeared in *Still in Song;* "Seen", "Shrimp", "Birthday" and "Tangled Vines" appeared in *Commonwoman;* "Woodcarver" appeared in *Conch.*

THE CANADA COUNCIL | LE CONSEIL DES ARTS
FOR THE ARTS | DU CANADA
SINCE 1957 | DEPUIS 1957

The Publisher gratefully acknowledges the support of
The Canada Council.

First Printing.

Dépôt légal, Bibliothèque Nationale du Québec and
The National Library of Canada.

Canadian Cataloguing in Publication Data

Goldberg, Marcia (Marcia Rajnus Goldberg)
    In mud season

1st ed.
Poems.
ISBN 0-921852-28-2

    I. Title.

PS8563.O8282315 1999   C811'.54   C99-901186-3
PR9199.3.S994I5 1999

The author wishes to thank Miriam Krant, Brian Nucci, Shloime Perel, Bede Urich, Amelia Houser, Gabi Tyrnauer and Burton Rubenstein, Brenda Epstein, Laura Fishman, Vivianne Silver, Georgette Pardo and Charles Stastny for human care and critical support over the last decade and longer as this book was finding its time to be. To Sonja and Geof for their bright encouragements, I cannot find ways to express my gratitude. To the McGill faculty who made my way plain, my words more worthy, I am not going to deny the great gifts of Darko Suvin, Leonore Lieblein, Abbott Conway, Yehudi Lindeman, Michael Bristol, Renée Karp and David Williams. In a category of their own, thanks to Roma Bross, Jerry Kazenal, Marie Dominic and Judy Yarnall. A special thanks to my students and co-reader/poet Rachael Bendayan at Vanier in my Dreamwork/Worldwork classes, who consented to be filmed at our "Dreaming Awake" reading in March of this year. To Nora Souskiassian, a very warm thank you for the final typing. And last, but far from least, I would like to add my deepest gratitude to my siblings, Lynda Siminski, Carla Rajnus, and Sara Drost, for their chatter in center field and cheering at all the bases.

CONTENTS

In Mud Season

Braced for a Different Deluge

Hot Teas

Kill Devil. Hills

In
Mud
Season

For Adam

PRELUDE

You make some kind of a choice,
light in the evening split on the snow
opening of the ark
or Pandora's box.

There you stand
married to the side of love
incomprehensible,
real space unbounded
on your skis, startled.

Had you been wearing snow shoes
it would have been no different.
The first step was a first step
and you made an effort to look up
into the night air darkening
where all that moisture
was molecules
you had to swallow
and their million trillion bits
you still face

at the edge of the Big Bay.

STIRRINGS

The terra cotta drip-dish catches
raindrops off lily-of-the-valley petals
pillowed on a mound of baby tear.
The dirt within goes red
at the splash of it. Rain.
The alchemy begins.

Rain drizzled from the roof eaves
Annoints and rewards your perspicacity.
You make alms by stirring the inch-deep pool.
Your stick seems bent as a brook
pushing over the smooth face of a boulder.

IN MUD SEASON

If you are out there where it happens,
everything slides, holds
to your soles, a kind of batter
that cannot nourish. You say to yourself,
"It's spring!" and "This heavy sticking into
will go by; this muck under dead grass
is thick with roots and seed;
sun *will* cut through. You will get out of it,
and under the cold leaves matted by snow
housing centipedes, sow bugs and ants
the loam is richer for another year
fed by these black stirrings."
Black and its dizziness
will be just another word
mixed as it *will* be with crocus
and poppy color. Wait until you see
the patterns sun makes! Taste
the fresh radish and find
in the continuous dark and light of waiting
the real reason: after the flood,
things catch and start. The work
is always in motion.

SIGNS

If you are hurt but have nothing to show,
how in the world as ice crawls to rock,
ice shoulders to rock, is anyone to know?

If life catches like quartz, okay, like snow
gone cold blue down to the soul rock,
if you are hurt but have nothing to show,

some striation where you were brought low
to register shock, betrayal, a benchmark,
how as ice shoulders to rock will we know?

Assume a disappointment, unwarranted blow,
a slash that your underbelly can't deflect.
How if you're hurt but have nothing to show

can the warmest hand dispatch even slow
to the cragged creature housed in the rock;
shouldered to ice, how is anyone to know?

When hope freezes under and heaves to and fro
in the bedrock when weather gets brisk,
if you are hurt but have nothing to show,
ice shoulders to rock; no one will know.

PARADOX LAKE FRAGMENT

I.   You step into wet mulch of lily pads when
allowing for miscalculations of the time
needed to balance in the sulphurating mud
you slip. Toes turn up the soft ooze;
the unflowered petioles of plants
mix furiously through the algae
but already you are gone, deeper
to where the cool depths of Paradox Lake
allow you a slippery footing.
You are toeing, chin deep. Your toe
gets a tenuous hold.
Under toe and along the shins,
lake perch nibble.

II.   Lake Paulinskill. The lake perch nibble
along your water-buried leg. The blond hair cillia
of your caterpillar stage. The blond head
bobbing by an inner tube. The white
legs and feet appearing by the rocks
unless the water moves. The birch legs
of your body with the wooden dock
mix up assurances of floating
so even sky sifting locust sounds
from tamaracks to stones that roll
gets mysterious and heavy
in its plucky veils.

III   Shades push out against the curtain
filling the dark room with scent of roses.
You dream of thunder clouds. You see
children catching lightning bugs in mayonnaise jars.
An earth smell. Wet grass. You sleep
with one leg on the rabbit's neck. On the black meadow

15

of your tranquil rest, cool air settles
over the barefoot children playing hide-and-seek,
and they forget to find you forever.
You watch the curious nightjar blink its tail.
The sound of Mother pulling the window down
brings your eyes open into the ink dark
where the rabbit is only another
invisible memory.

PRESENCE

I am not alone. A cat bathes on my knee;
a child sleeps in a room. A boy
dreams of his day. My thoughts
are left for the night. Prayer
or meditation or language
lets off its shoes. They fall
by the thousands. I will hear them
as I sleep
and think of the man who wept
because he had no shoes
until he met a man who had no feet.

The rainbow, you said, is a sign
G-d gave there would be no more floods
until the fire. Four times I looked across the field today
for the end of the rainbow. Simple arithmetic:
the multiplication of assurances —
no more destruction by flood.

DELILAH/SCHEHERAZADE

I am a poet
all marbled and veiled —
the roads I have journeyed
reveal no end —
trees, bridges, fencing and hills
pull a line on the top.
I am grown colder
(a veil disappears without a sound).
Days tan and gray, pink
settle into patterns.
The trees bud, sprout and fall
(behind the veil coins jingle,
the belly is certainly involved).
A car swerves over into my lane.
Bills arrive. Hesitation rides
on a job application.
Immutable events become rock.
A tiny cymbal rings at my fingers.

WINTER HOME

I have spent my time running on the beach,
pulling the small shape of the baby upon my back.
Tracked pipits out to the sea. Shouldered
waiting hours, under the sun. The sand
was still friendly then. It gave up shells,
wood bits. We played with worm-burrowed rocks
and strung tackle and buoys, coral and shale.
Infinite Sand, Benefactor, I have felt your heat.

This cold cabin which houses us, now
without you, straddles a rockier earth, pelted with rain.
School now carries the child. My back
still bends some. The sand we have known
is pebbles here. The stones roll from their banks
and slide under our feet. Leeched time and safety/tumble together.
The sun cowers in the slate sky. What, Sky, Mentor,
is the direction you would take us?

FLIGHT

Who said you could do this work?
The sheep line up, the cows line up.
You look around the country
like a larger bird, an owl
or a hawk, perched visibly
atop a pine. When the wind blows,
you do not buckle or bend,
but as you leave a branch,
your pleasure is immediate.
This gives you the right
and does not disturb the others.

PROPOSAL(S)

Light may be moved
in ways we won't expect.
This morning
a thunderhead
milky as smoky quartz under amethyst
rumbled up on the horizon
where Natalie saw deer
grazing this time yesterday
in that scarcely settled place;

     now it's gone, too,
     like fiery foliage
     spied thru onyx glass
     displayed at leaded panes,
     beveled and diamond-cut,

          or, perhaps, more snappy,
          like a blue swirled globe,
          a manganese double-bubble
          inside a small snail paperweight
          someone's just lifted.

WINSLOW

Just one stroke in watercolour, the tree goes to paper;
black runs to grey. Dries. The webbing
and veining of twigs to the sky,
single leaf dropped, freeze in the mind.
Colour and where it should go,
the rutting of maple bark, the jut of the forked branch,
realization top leaves are stripped —
fifteen clumps of yellow
might suggest the total —
or is it the wind,
how it shuffles the light to the eye?

CAMEL'S HUMP

I have left the summit and am dug in
under an unnamed ridge for the winter.
That's part of it. The fact that my real trek
ended at noon does not disqualify my thought:
"The poet creates his own imaginary world," Jack said.
We had just come off
someplace called the lion
that I thought said the loin on the map.
Cutter said, "Sure," with a laugh,
"We traversed right under the tail," and I smiled.
But in my mind I am still maybe in Beaver Meadow
after the group and the snowmobiles have left. No,
farther up and off, it would have to be.
Identify the unmarked trees and uncut firewood.
I can still sometimes hear a Vulcan gun.
(Once I thought from my lodge
I could see someone camping above me.
It was only the moon severed by clouds
and mixed in the spruce.)
The thrum of the truck taking
cartons to Stowe is too muffled a sound for my ear.
I do not see out or beyond my hat. I have dropped
into a gully. When the wind blows here
I know that the trek is over, and I can get down
by myself whenever I want.
The ridges, the gaps,
the chill and the snow
invite me to stay for the winter;
the ice walls I slid down to find myself here
are a jumble with proofs and figures, confused lines
I am going to stay and think out.

SHRIMP

I was more dubious than anyone
mail ordering sea monkeys, *Artemia
salina,* the shrimp
to be birthed miraculously from packet No. 2
three days after the salt dissolved, tinier
than swimming gnats and just as clownish.
I would have thrown them out for dead,
a bad deal, on the second day,
but you, believing,
would not let me, said I didn't dare
take *one life* until the six weeks passed
the Emergency Instructions directed us to wait!

Now I see how they have grown, nearly to a quarter inch,
swim on their spines and spin their tiny legs.
For amusement, I note in the guide from Flushing,
New York, how they breathe from their feet,
mate in forcible play, kill,
in rambunctious masses
if the diet is tuned to their liking.

I would have dumped this dwarfish world,
presumptuous in all its demands, cataloguing
silly performances creatures can be made to do
under lights, would have blanked the whole experiment,
handily. And now the aquarium's swirling
with hundreds of guests, you have lost interest,
little jester. Was it for this   —
to prove with a cartoon offer
how brilliant the littlest are?

THE HUMMINGBIRDS AT COARSEGOLD

The guest bed held me afloat
in my sister's sister-in-law's home
past noon, the feeders, red-capped and filled
with sugary suspension, all being readied
as I fought away a fever, so that now,
sun pressing on the overcast air mass,
cool summer breeze wafting perfume of oak,
coos of mourning doves, I sit here on the redwood deck
closer to thirty or forty hummingbirds
arriving overhead from the pink mimosa,
some solo pilots off the cedars,
than I have ever sat before, so close, in fact,
that they seem to care very little if my prying eyes
want to fix their form here or there.

The *Selasphorus rufous* has not come back
with its tangerine tail fanned,
this lover of alpine meadows, the edges
of Yosemite woodlands, who flies farther north
than any other hummingbirds
and whirls in mountains thirteen thousand feet up,
breeding in colonies of nests just two feet apart.
Anna's hummingbirds, metallic green or red crested,
like the black chinned-variety, fork-tailed
and bordered with iridescent purple who congregate
in pendulumlike arcs, court
in what now is beating heat as lunch is served indoors.

Outdoors, a woodpecker works on the scrub brush,
the beaked twitters and winged hums around my straw hat
make me a Vincent Van Gogh, dizzied, no mathematician,
by a California garden where
thirty hidden hummingbirds swap places with the thirty seen,

25

tweeting and twittering over the sound
of a rotating sprinkler, levitate
an inch or two above the four tall feeders
with stations that accommodate a dozen at a time.
One, I force myself to notice, sips six draughts
before it shuttles off. How much
is six dips at twelve stations times four
if the lovers quarrel over everything, the nearby grosbeak,
orioles, American goldfinches, flickers, nuthatches, and creepers
just two yards off on my right
move, too, in the hovering dance?

MONTREAL LANGUAGE

This downpour shakes and splashes Your name
across the polished umbrella over the picnic table
in rivulet-streamers, chases down the winding staircase
and splotches my page written in thunder, pulls me back
to the fresh hills of Lyndonville where,
as no other word rhymes with *month,* I found no language
for mud puddles overrunning the concrete slabs
like the ones on our sixplex walkway. The steady drizzle today
while I'm dragging in the mundane chaise lounge, soaked flatout,
carries me back, asks for the name of the way my kitten prowls,
for the model of how this work began in the first place,
whether I am ready to begin this day speaking
behind pink impatiens, blood red geraniums
on the empty summer balcony
since no place at all is ever really empty.

WHAT TO LEAVE BEFORE THE HOUSESITTER COMES

Book order, short story collections, library acquisitions,
mark update, module, insurance policy letter, check
for veterinarian, the movers, cat food, rug and laundry matters,
the film. Then the light touching neon yellow day lily
posed halfway up the trunk of birch
near the chain-link gate, asphalt ruelle,
ivy-covered wooden fence of neighbours who trap squirrels
and whom I've never met, probably never will,
screams for calm, and I see that.

THE NIGHT I LEFT CLASS

The moon on a blazed blue sky
blue as an oyster in shade
the moon a pearl on an oyster
shiny on a blue table cloth
the trees, branches
off center in a spray
the moon a sprayed drop
off center in a purple wave
a handblown bubble
white as milkglass, clear fostoria
the moon all bubbled and pressed
bright enough the ring
for its own vase of iris.

BLOOM

Yesterday it had not opened;
satin crimson bowl today,
it threw those petals
wide as an amusement park ride
throwing all of us with it
in outraged relief.

Yesterday, we had wanted that poppy burst
from its tightly fitted husk,
scarcely coloured but for the hint of scarlet
forbidding us even a guess
about what it would take —
showers, sleep, soil up to its chin next season. . . .

Today, this spider-centered fact
retracts nothing:
white-flecked at the core overnight,
huge eye on the firmament,
stars and clouds and what
dramatizes
the center of red light curiosity
 — the hard truth —
done, given, possible.

HOW THEY PIECED TOGETHER

(from Elinor Pruitt Stewart's *Letters*)

She said they used scraps
at Christmas. Trudging sixty miles
into a cañon, they strung paper birds on human hair,
cut and re-sewed a blanket into a slip for the new mother;
it took her thoughts from unemployment.

They made candelabra from the partial jars at their disposal.
With this lighting, taking only whiskey and morphine,
she hacked off a man's finger on a block of wood
and saved his life, dousing the open vein.
It involved only a small trick of distraction.

When the squalling baby hollered, her daughter explained,
"The angels sent it to us." Since they "weren't no angels,"
said Mrs. Stewart, they kept him, laughing
in her emphasis, roasting the antelope,
stirring the butter, sure of her power to help.

THRASHING

(for Gabriela Mistral)

I am in blue two shades of blue
sitting in a school a teacher's room
my child's away no man this job
is temporary you Remind me
to knit sweaters. I clip with you
six small cotton diapers. I fold
each one. Now my pain is ready
to be quiet. The child in me is seeds
but I am elm my branch moves
and the sky knows in me the roots.

BLACK BEE

Completely contented not to shop at the flea market
I take out the basket of grapes,
sit on the hood of the car,
and listen to the airplane and crickets,
the radios and highway traffic
intruding upon the acres of grass.

Four tear-shaped seeds
then two, yellow and lavender,
with a thin orange detail near the tip
from the grape I suck away,
from skin, pull off the meat of Concord.

A woman in a white sailor cap
handles the cups of plants
wrapped in aluminum foil
wondering, I suppose,
about the stroke she mentioned having.

Somewhere at a table far afield, a silver bell rings.
Four more seeds, then three, spill to my hand
and this sweet-sour grape, the last day of summer this year,
stays in my mouth for a moment
as you return, arms full,
like the purple clover to the small black bee.

SHEER FLAMINGO

I dream of the gateway to Honolulu's Zoo
where turquoise paint borders mossy shallows
in a picture-perfect South Pacific park;
palm frond, melon-coloured shower tree, and rosy proteus
surround more than fifteen pink flamingos,
each standing on one thin leg, sunning necks rolled back
and pronated bills tucked behind a wing
leaving just pink tufts on poles with triple digit feet
like candy dandelions in a dream garden

except for one who leads a group
close to me and my small party,
eyeing us with a pale yellow eye,
then backing off, hibiscus tinge of pink.
It mixes with the staves of ginger, stalks of bird of paradise,
local horn-billed ibis, till it sees fit
to wander back, closer to the gate,
regarding us as if it wants to dance,
sees we really can't leap or leave the fence,
and without craning its neck,
without hop or hesitation, rolls,
so to speak, in a fluid, toy-like motion,
right down the slope to its artificial pond
and dips the back of its elegant, black-tipped beak,
into the warm, wet water, winks.

Uprooting Causes of War

It was an accidental harvest
after the first frost, at a time when hands move quickly
out-of-doors, anticipating wet things
sliding beneath the leaves, and a time when
summer's wealth seems to be slipping elsewhere,
forgetting all kinds of human poverty.

We must have thought that we were the center
of the universe. A black cat mask, spinning witness,
swung lightly on a line. A loaded delphinium
drooped over the work site
where the mishap sparked a confrontation.

This will be a hurried cleansing, I thought;
purging the lawn of clots of leaves had been difficult.
Ivy and berry vines clutched the rusted rake under flower beds;
then, the rake broke like a cracked ramrod. Unstoppable,
I started after dry fronds under fern, grabbing clumps
soft as hair, hand to hand, in rapid-fire succession.

With wicked thoroughness, I launched a further assault
after wizened pumpkin vines. Just visiting my sister's land,
I ripped vines from roses, sorted the lot, divided
and chopped graying bolts depleted by the cold,
and severed four bare-pated globes —
everything my sister had, in the way of pumpkins.

Things that green need a chance to ripen, I laughed miserably
as my sister came to praise my work. I saw confusion first;
she buried hurt and outrage quicker. She did note, though,
how I'd taken all her crop, set pumpkins slashed at the wick
on the porch, and heard me say I hadn't meant it.

She wasn't saying what
lay below the surface
when she took my laughter the wrong way.
Wednesday the heat-repairman's bumper read: "Commit
Random Acts of Kindness." I mention this, because
we feuded night and day in silence,
cold hostility robbing me of sleep.

Time, of course, could not have been one iota briefer.
We held few remaining cards to play, years out of touch, a week
to negotiate our losses. I would not say "fortunately,"
but for some reasons we did not fully understand,
in my sister's house, each day we drew an angel card
with one word on the back, tiny, slick,
overturned on a wicker tray.

In this case, before the incident on foreign turf dismembered
what there was of soul and psyche,
I noted when I rose on Friday,
she had drawn a card before she went to work. The word
that she'd turned up was "Peace."
I took one too, wanting *strength* that day
or *wisdom,* to place beside her solace-giving choice.
The word I drew from the angel basket and placed
on Mother's table, for us to see that night, was "Love."

KISS THE BOOFER LADY;
TEXT FOUND ON A BOOKMARK

(for Allen Ginsberg)

Kiss the Boofer Lady:
a book, perhaps? Entitled by a gangster?
A mystery, but what about the woman
in her slippers, her hairpins, rollers,
crackers in her sofa, cat hairs,
the vacuum and the light bulb?
What's she doing with the laundry?
Do we know her? Has she been out?
What's she eating, saving, sorting, shooing from the porches,
taking in for hungry, putting down? What's she smelling?
What's she doing with the string, the waxes, candles;
are there groceries? Was she once called Kitty?
Was she married? Did she have to?
Have a fur coat? Have a brandy?
Was she slow to start to speak?
At what age *did* she first sit up?
Could she take the metro from Decarie
down to Cote St. Catherine reminding Mother
of the dollar in the cabinet by the floorlamp where they'd put it
for a movie just for such occasions? Do we know
she was a *bear* for putting on the dog? What *was* her language
when she took her shirt off, drew the bath
and poured the pitcher of sour milk into the toilet
because the tenement had roaches and her husband
would not be home till later, much, much later?
Just who *do* we think she was? And to *kiss*
is a tall order if her head was filled with brown bag lunches
where the cleric lost a punch line;
what did she know of Ruth or of the Angels?
Was her card game ever used?
Did she read tea leaves, dust the ashtrays, even smoke?

How many afternoons in blistering heat did she come
north from Rio to attend a lecture on transcendental meditation
in the winter of the Seven Wars against her doctor's orders?
Kiss her? Whom did she kiss? Lord knows the lunchroom
offers more encumbrance than the stockpile
or the dockyard, but was she ever down there by the pilings
where the cats twist their long and sultry necks towards
small noises? Did she wash the dishes? Kiss her?
Pet the pony? Ride the needle to the top without a look back?
Was she winning? Was it Bingo? Was her pattern ever checkered?
What I want to know is if the Plaza or the Ritz
collided in her head with the Chelsea? Did she lace
a baby's boots and take a satchel with her nightgown
and a toothbrush to Chicago when she hiked last year to Dallas?
Make the Astros look her over? Did she play there?
Then it must have been her stage name? What's this gasping?
Is she crying? Has she taken cold? Does she have a Kleenex?
In the Alfa Romeo? By the swimming pool — she wasn't even
swimming — did you see her? Kiss her? In black clothes —
I have to stop myself from guessing —
in *black* clothes with a white collar:
there is a reason for the way she dresses.
I know when she spells Balzac she finds her old Larousse
and she balances downhill on ice the way a woman
rather like her may have told a secret
to just one other in the room —
it could have been the Boofer Lady —
a thing that left her speechless,
utterly speechless,
and she would have liked to have a kiss.

FROGS AT MUD CREEK

Approaching the pond at Mud Creek,
I drive frogs from ground cover — black striped, yellow-eyed,
dark green like grass snakes —
but each unperturbed dragon-fly clutches a blade
in rhythmical turquoise dissent.

Like Monet, I want to paint the lagoon, deeply shadowed
and darkening, and its water lilies —
referring to details I can almost name,
— vine-like foliage mixed with cattails, hedge
beyond scrub oak, — but I have to move down closer.

Four frogs hop up from the fern;
one settles on pond scum eyeing me like Midas,
wishing to paralyze my progress.

A breeze ripples a belt of water in a broad stroke of blue
beyond the lilies. A footbridge makes me think
of a medieval, long-breathed "amen"; a cottonwood tree
turns its gray underside with a brush of beige.
One move closer pries two bright, wet frogs from the weeds
into the petals of perfect white lilies floating like candle cups.

If I stand, I worry, so close to the rushes (it's almost a blind),
will anything stir? Muskrats swim at sunset from here,
kingfishers pair, and ducks dart in the greens.
I do stand, and like that, the shock of a great blue heron
blurs over my right shoulder; the water slightly adjusts itself
as I lean forward, notice clusters of frog's eggs
thickening the matted edge, then
great sacks of frog's eggs
as I plunk myself down.

Six more tiny green frogs
leap to defend their water homes.

Did Monet ever get so close to the burrs? I wonder.
Racing to the general pastel spectacle, my heart
hurries away from the thrill of electric chartreuse.
Two late frogs sneak up behind me and hurry past,
drive me from Mud Creek cowed by their confidence.

ORIGINS

In January, I took the skate egg
palm up to the burst black pod,
corner pockets tipping up and down
with four elongate-tentacles
whipping like skates themselves I'd seldom seen
and at my feet in the sand found
my first all amber hula lei band, a whelk strand,
like a plunged wax straw case
curling bulbously, unlike
those hard little whelk shells, unlike
any beginnings I'd have thought, unlike
my first guesses at where I'd come from
out of uterine foam whence I'd skated and dined,
got through college and jobs, whelped and resigned,
unlike what even now I'd recognize as the female tissue
that tucked around and spawned me into
my own early days that I could never have guessed
until I discovered another placenta,
gone now forever, and said:
Ah, yes, from this sapiens satchel
spins out human form, casts up
the flailing and form-finding spirit
of shelled and skittering human habitants
into this fishpond-ocean earth.

BIRTHDAY

I was in labour all night and the next day with my first child
ready, I thought, for anything (which is the way
I prefer to think before waves crest up and get snarly),
but all I remember through those twenty-three hours
besides the functional facts
between superior clinches and contractions
of fetal monitor and periodic checks
by the medical student in charge
because my doctor was driving up from the Cape
and the way people milled in and out of the room
like guests at a disappointing banquet (indeed,
I felt the festival air and held forth once or twice
with a bawdy phrase, a try at Bacchanalian jabber,
and only once heaved a frustrated retch, dry, into a silver plate
and after that was given only a lemony swab to suck)

all I can remember
as on a strained postcard
thin over the river Charles and reverting
to an extraterrestrial peace
pink over Boston from my saddle-safe table
under white sheets like a confused customer awake and asleep
while dilation arrested and someone suggested drugs —
"No drugs!" I commanded — and pitocin began to drip,
then I swerved into gyrating intervals
more physical than climbing Big Moose
and my husband, an intern, stood there
waiting as if he expected a newspaper to be delivered and
an anesthesiologist came to hypnotize me back
into "Breathe, press, relax"—
was this one thing:

I remember after we moved to the other room
where mirrors and lights bounced with skin flashes
of thigh, belly, face
how seriously gay it felt to touch bottom of the life mass
I never understood till the moment you flooded Earth
into the proper room,
cheering, yes, and even in the squall got out and up in my
arms,
your dad touched speechless except
for the absurdly beautiful remark
I think I heard him make —
(Something) how really cool —
(Something, Something) and I, as I say,
touching bottom, touched,
and alive!

Dorion in a Bar

This Dutch guy. So fat,
he had to pick up the vinyl chair
and put it on the couch beside him
so he'd have space to warm his legs
by the pot-bellied stove. Said
he's been over here about eight days,
but spoke clear English. Businessman,
and hard to see, facing ahead toward the bar.
He knew I knew something he needed to know,
but I needed to know who he was, and I didn't.
Pretty soon, he decided to try again,
pulling his big elbow, so awkwardly hooked
on the edge of the vinyl chair, off
into a more natural pose.
Sitting up a little on the rich, crushed velvet,
he talked at last about classical music.
I said, "All modern music isn't flat; look at Prokofiev,"
and he asked me what I thought of Dvorak:
"More melody than Prokofiev," I said. "Oh, yes,
all you could want," the Dutchman said.
Funny you should say that, I thought,
catching his face in the little flame
flooding my eyes despite multiple chins like a river
flowing northward, softly, in a spring melt till his ardent eyes
connected the lines of one passionate, angry chin.
Next day, this Dutch guy appears. Three piece suit,
different room, looking larger and older.
I turned to my friend to ask if she knew who he was.

AFTER ALL WARS

Wherever I go, I nearly overstep:
behold! The gray tree frog, clinging
to the fern stalk, the common poor-will,
nestled in stony camouflage,
the blue jay young, unable to fly,
the marsh marigold, perishable, perishable.

WAY TO GLOVER

So this is freedom —
the caravan moving by Caspian Lake
past ridges of yarrow,
groves of maples in dazzling sun.
How little we know, joined along whispering roads,
where the locusts in cedars
and the day, even approaching Shadow Lake,
the little cemetery on the green hills,
takes us. The Domestic Resurrection Circus
in the middle of August begins en route.
All of us select our way through Craftsbury,
Eden or Woolcott, our universal metaphor:
this deciding to drive
through gray birch and pines
dropping to flowered banks when we finally arrive
where we think we'll see something —
an event at the amphitheater
leaping with biting grasshoppers
and reliable versions of dance.

Chancing on the Subject of Dress Outside The Now Bankrupt Company Store

Before February hearts and flowers,
a new peasant dress; Who
does she think she is? Parading before May
in paisley, buying cotton in the freezing,
looking pleased in knee-high calfskin
like a princess in expensive
peasant dress, possibly
she will forget this nonsense,
get back to work.
Oh, she could,
but later, preening, putting on a peevish peasant slouch
and turning sideways, she thinks,
I like it. I think it becomes me.
It is becoming you.
You are becoming poor, unpleasant,
unpleasing in your crushed *paruschka,*
too pale skirt and blouse,
improper for the winter, billowing
big in your skirts,
Heavens!

DARTH VADER CLIFFS

To this we have come,
the lake gully so cold the little ones
curl in the crevices. Among chipped stones
under drumming waves
on the ice-shard coast in the yowl and blast
of the east, we discover one of our own
coiled on a ledge in fetal position.

Our cave objective hindered by beast droppings,
cork-screw roots, wet rock handholds and a hum,
on the windy side, of mechanical breathings,
we work past the holes of sand creatures,
eyes of newts, quick motion of frog,
up the cuff to the field.

At last on a tractor-cut swath,
we call through fallen leaves
until we find a wider range.
The Force comes to grips with the frozen lake.
The snow holds back a few more days.
As the company divides
to search the woods for its wrappings,
I lie back on cornstalks
to skywrite.

MANUFACTURING FORTUNES
FOR COOKIES

At a vegetarian restaurant in Chinatown,
we dream them up: the ghost
you do not know really likes you;

You will have a great future in darts;
You will meet a friend who loves "purnips";
You were meant to be a Great Carrot farmer.

There is a vegetal progression:
You'll have an urge to make spaghetti sauce for thousands;
You will make a fortune in fortune cookies;

You have a future in bowling. We keep, because we did this,
You may fly past fireworks before morning,
and I supply, continue as you read this poem!

LETTER FROM HOME

You are out of the jungle crossing the grass
like Scarlett O'Hara coming up slowly:
Hello Hello you say to no one at all.
You pass the arboretum palms wondering dubiously,
Have they really been pulled to earth
and snapped upright again? The carp
pocket themselves around the lagoon
while you step to the marble porch
of the Queen Ann Cottage and stare
from the spacious veranda over the water.
Behind you, a mirror, a music box,
a porcelain doll. Transported,
you watch the Indians bring the dinner up
from the Reid adobe, as if you have lived here,
curried your horses.

Was that you? Was that ever you?

Knock at the carriage house of your heart
paneled with mahogany, founded
on floorboards swept and washed
where the drain slats are; or walk
to the Victorian mansion, up to the cupola;
wait by the water
until the canoes set out. Let the thunder
remind you, resonant whinnies. The ginkgo tree
drops its fanned-heart leaves.

It is a small and pinched arboretum,
shrinking or perhaps now shrunk, but then
it was all great space around a eucalyptus eighty feet tall,
fallen into a primeval forest
where you were the unicorn and all around

that was, was fossil fern, dense azaleas,
first plant life and gaseous flaming,
streams of green, green-gray,
and browns of fertile soil for growing corn.
You fed the ducks, found peacock feathers
those last times searching to know over and over
the center of yourself
which sang and had no limits.

Acres and acres of bamboo, thorny *polyboracho,* oleander
and day lilies move their forms and stories,
their perfumes lingering even forty years after
so nothing you can say can disprove
how the *Tally Ho* came rolling past the herb garden,
six drays pulled by thoroughbreds
shaking their manes in the California heat,
or how you knew the Mestizos dresses so thoroughly
bringing the morning bread. You watched their banded hair
mirrored like a painting in the pond.
The last pond left.
Leaning near the aviary by the coach house
yards from the Queen Ann Cottage,
you spun your antebellum notions
guessing how the sloshy swamp these natives poled
was homeland once when water wet the planet for trilobites,
the lanky brontosaurus —
creatures marked for giant grace —
and tumbled with them
watching turtles dive.

WHERE KILLARNEY ENDS

Seldom Seen Road and *Blind River*
read the signs along the highway
crossing Canadian shield and outcroppings
near the Spanish River and tiny village of Webbwood.

Two weeks later,
Wayne Gretzky and Michael J. Fox get married,
one to a woman in a forty-thousand dollar gown
who's gifted with a Rolls Royce white convertible,
the other, in Arlington, Vermont,
in an unidentified neighbourhood.

Here in Webbwood, a tire suspended on a rope from a tree
looks small enough to ornament a model train town.
"Lionelville," Judy says, and while I'm musing
over the town marked *East Pronto* not on the map, my voice
is drowned out by pneumatic chisels.

Past Serpent River Reservation
we examine beads, leather, and wood,
catch a first glimpse in blazing sun of Lake Huron.
It is hard to think about or remember our small resources
already heading back, in some sense, mindfully,
across tracks that won't be nearly quite these
before we even reach the conference,
this long road in friendship mostly what we came for.

SEEN

By the Greyhound station
he spun off the curb carrying the child
under his arm like a bunch of sticks,
his shoulders big as a woodsman's;
and when the buses revved their engines,
he started running,
his yellow ringlets flying,
grizzled and twisted like a troll's,
and she, a little Kettlehead
tucked into a red snow suit,
watched sideways,
her blue eyes excited at the turn.
He ran in his big boots,
head moving left to right, checking the traffic.
The asphalt street became a forest,
and I saw him steal that girl
for his dinner.

WOODCARVER

Woodcarver, he say, good
in butternut carve careful;
sign needs ease for eye
where chipped, grooved recess
meet the letter. Cut perfect,
he say, and show me tools
wood-handled with grooved
steel, folded in soft leather.
Say clear-edged alphabet
cut best if cut with care
but not edged too straight 'cause
eye need roundness, curve
need way to wobble with
recess texture, need fun way
blend together reading, carving,
curving, so even sign
connect pleasure in the greeting,
while I smile how he go
stoutly to the door, leave me
feel curve made by his roundness
in little room, clear relief
form against bottle glass ripple,
swirl of cottage prism,
go away smiling, bunched vest neat.

AFTER THE OLYMPICS, 1994

Some are asking for more troops in Sarajevo;
some are looking for a way to arm the Muslims or Croats.

Here in Westmount, we're having bitter sunshine, variable clouds.
Here we see light glare silently across our snowy yards

as if grasses soon grow green and bulbs take flower,
as if trees soon bud abundantly and bloom.

Talks of peace through violated ceasefires,
talks of UN aid to starving victims

seem far from ivies and from sunny spider plants my cats attend,
seem simple as forgetting where we've put the minutes.

A phone call away from disaster? A quiet garden. . .
a phone call away from gunfire? Deforestation?

A fence away from Sniper Alley? Putting war into it —
a fence capped with snow topiaries the wind made —

Some pent-up preparation, like La Bomba's dash* —
some abstract misconduct slips; some awfully dismal failure speeds

wide of its marks as the gaze of disbelief
widens on the nature of sport.

* Reference to Alberto Tomba, Italian silver medalist in men's slalom,
who came back from twelfth place in a "miracle finish."

LENS

Tomorrow will be lovelier if we look at it with today's eyes,
because today's eyes saw how much we had not seen.

Watch life.
Don't write about it.
Yet the cryptic eye
Catches, gets a glimpse,
Wants to close on the action.
No iris but ours
Has lavished its sight
Exactly here before.

The camera finds Harvey
stroking Lisa's hair. Breast. Hair.

Write it down
Don't write about it
Watch life
Write it down.

Braced For a
Different
Deluge

CETUS, UNFOLDING

She has a silver star
sunken in her eyes
(I didn't know it was about stars
I would write whose suns
cast a warmer light
from those tranquil places
which are her eyes than the ordinary
glass cold twinklers in the starry mass
surrounding surrounding the usual sky.)
The rare glow
like her own motioning and highlit hair
kicks up spots of dynamite drama.
(I remember those eyes
when she was a child. The star
was showing then, too, in the landscape
of undying invitations.)
One good contact stare into that soul struck
into by the silver star in her eyes
pours in something none of us knows about
heavenly orbs. For age there is none.
There is a lingering attachment. There is
a fixed but dancing
Artistry that laughs at death
and heats my solitary, sky-whipped heart.

GRANDFATHER'S SHOP

Grandfather's shop huddled in bricks
except where the lathe was;
there he had boards cut into curls
(I never saw the inside part;
it was the cold porch I recall
where Grandma draped covers on chairs)
and Grandpa made bowls,
little pumps that were lamps and
bowls that fit together like jigsaw puzzles;
he had hundreds of his own inventions
like sewing box rockers my grandmother covered with cushions
and alphabet blocks and toys and furniture for dolls.
Now I in my thirty-first year
have too a shop of a sort in my home,
the finished products out for inspection —
mirrors with miniature trains in their margins,
ornaments and, alphabet blocks
like Grandpa's, but flatter,
and bakers on barn boards and books done in dough
strung out in baskets and boxes
awaiting as much as my Grandfather's wares
a buyer, a beggar, a user who cares.

ON LAKE IROQUOIS

I went fishing today and got
sunburned and bottle-capped.
By that I mean, the sun had a way
of keeping its distance like wolves
prowling around
and the aspen carr where the black snakes are
shifted its multi-million roots and peat droppings
silently under its water-láppèd feet
(little reedy feet that whistled with their unseen bird-mouths).
Chiirup, chiirup I think I heard the pikes announcing
but they kept their distance under the boat
so the pressure of wanting some things
that are as far-away and unbearable
in the way they are never deciphered —
like midget minnows writing their names
in the hot mossy waters off limestone rocks —
That pressure baking in the shook up bottle
that ferments in my frothy mind, rolling
with the waves, such as they were,
smallish, but not without their hitches,
got snarled and tangled and then
(almost the very moment I reeled in
and found *potamogeton* tendrils had bent the pole taut
till the line sprang loose in a gust from the wind)
I found out... my needs and my didn't needs
married in the spermy cloud bed pushing back and forth,
and the half-heat of my desire to catch *something*
poked under my oar, pulled on my pole,
pumped up some sunshine, and fizzed
softly as salmon eggs, stuck in their sweetly oil

BIRD

The single-wattled cassowary
is a stuck belly dancer.
She — solitary as a diamond,
but delft- and snake-belly blue at the neck —
hangs alone
with ostrich hips awaddle,
halted, but no slow come-ons,
because the cassowary,
whether it's the toenail-like wattle
where the veils should be,
or the potato-thick legs
that stalk the ground instead of
small ankled, happy-toed soul ladders,
does not want to tangle,
and so its gown gets plumed out
at the tails and its feathers
sheik-up at the neck,
do not go together
nor attract.
It is a stuck bird
and despises the dance.

ORISON

Gray dot crosses the rain flap
past my sheltered legs. Arms extended, "fingers" afold,
on the thin yellow tent roof,
it stops: Daddylonglegs!
It is the longest day of the year.

At sun up, you are saying of our Creator
the importance of each brilliant detail
keeping laughter
at the fundament
of this trek.

POINT TO CROSSING

We travelled into the border town like a pinball
pinging into the glitter; the piñata burst
into a city of decorated clay and paint,
little gifts, ringing up lights; the street lights
slower than a pull-pin drawing out against
the spring. Hours before the curve-wending auto
and its charges slowed down — the narrow escapes
in the marketplace (low whistles and *pan y tequila,*
brilliant paper flowers six-for-a-dollar en *mano de niño*
and the Conquistador Glass Works)
stopped spinning from hubcaps —
we raced unpaved roadways, stopping and starting.

The shanties sprocketed with late-noon reflections
on metal slats caught at the sun
flashing off clap-trap walls, beaming like silver wands,
and we had to cross pot-holes past barbed wire fence
without warning, running full force together,
the three of us, ditching our fugitive feeling
right at the edge of that time-pressing confluence
where channels and histories
pour into the darting and bucketed sea.

NOTE FROM THE VAULT

from *The Book of Mechanical Parts*

The accoutrements of the workplace —
coffee cup, felt-tip markers —
meshed with familiar sounds —
the radio, sprocketed with advertising.
It is so private a world,
nobody sees it. Nobody hears
the man at his desk, sneezing.

But I do. I think Denise does, too.
I think Bob and Beth do, across their spaces
on the plastic carpet shielding.
Steve does. He catches me off guard
demonstrating the adjustable triangle.

The cardboard crate is stabbed
by unbent hangers, cross-hatched and numbered
to provide a rolled-map file.
Joining together the Polar Planimeter
while seated on metal stool by the draftboard,
I catch a tiny world with a small vocabulary
like special intelligence.

You are to work in a windowless place
says the dropped hammer in the attic.
You collapse like a sheaf of paper,
recoil like a telephone cord.
Like a pocket watch, wind and unwind.
Like a typewriter ribbon, roll from reel to reel.
Nothing is magic.

Outside, and across the street
the granite edifice washed last week
gleams with the clarion chimes
while eight desks are wheeled to the walls
each one becoming more invisible.

But I see them. I think Ed does, too.

AT THIS CORNER AGAIN:
ANOTHER NUMINOUS PLACE

I've been told to look for "the white water";
more dutiful than attentive, or more fortunate
I've found this section of stream again
which lies still with its mosses all summer
but in spring it forgets itself, cuts rock
under a bridge of cement — a snow slope runs into
this gulch: it mixes me up.

Seeing the curl in the middle
where a rock or log sets up a dead man's noose
(this is no fairy land) am I, despite the mud running,
not a pioneer sitting on the toothed slab writing?
Or, if I release the control, is this not the Ice Age
back, dumping a visible portion
of all there is? Imagine sitting on this rock
longer than half an hour, pitted over time,
licked, fractured, and oh! — pioneer!
made to watch change within and without.

So if it comes back to the self,
this looking,
realize then only some of it,
in a sense, is distracted,
splashed to a beam or lost to air.
White water coiling 'round stone on the borders
(though dried milkweed and straw
catch on thorns in the fissures) bears
a certain undistracted force, alive
together with the rest of the world,
or just in its own body,
a certain incomprehensibility,
but swift, this cavern.

67

TANGLED VINES

for Lyn Lifshin

Daughter, we were told
was the common name of the orange tuberous
weed like a deadly potato eye strangling
the ivy bed. My mother
could have been a botanist
the way she studied plants —
gloxinia, bottle bush, bonsai, calla lily —
though she had no fond regard
for the parasite.
She had four daughters herself
and understood, when my father could not hinder
the vegetable tendrils carried by spores
down from the gray and arid Sierra Madres
by daily weeding or spraying,
that it was time to get the experts.
It bothered me to name a weed the thing
we were, daughters,
as if it made a problem of us, too,
and to have my mother stare placidly
through the livingroom window
across the rising yard to the ivy,
then up to the mountains "From whence,"
she often said, "cometh our help"
while outside the *daughter*
was finally poisoned,
cleanly stripped by the gardener
from all that lush and miniaturized greenery,
as iris yellow grows away from stem.

SEASONS AT LAKE CARMI

We camped under a clear sky
swept by constellations. My son
never spoke of the Milky Way
eroding the firmament;
in tracing a satellite
minutely travelling through space,
I saw the torpedo-tailed blackbird
solo in its trajectory.
When the child fell into sleep
perfumed by cedar and swamp, I watched a meteor
fall twice across the pond.
Would my boy sleep the night, I wondered,
detaching myself from the effluence of spring
night, perfect disorder
of the prismatic universe. . . .

We slept in the mushrooming nylon bags
exposed on the grass beach like grubs:
the birds no longer worked, nor the waterfowl,
nor did the fish splash. Our rounded feet
faced the granite-edged depths
like monuments.

In a fit of dreaming, my eyes opened
on the treed isle
like a stranger. The distant farms
on the groomed hills had vanished. The split moon
hacked half the pines to white. In a brief span,
we had come to winter. Gray light on a starless field
filtered and covered the nocturnal creatures.
Two fish surfaced under the water,
drawing luminous lavender lines
parallel to shore. The child slept
through the cutting of glass.

I moved fitfully then.
Had it not been for the thundering June bugs
in the cut weed, I might have missed
the swift strokes of the third
transformation.

My eyes opening under the violet flap
conveyed me by rickshaw around the dim expanse.
Two ducks, black as messengers, flashed past
in a patch of lighted trees,
charging the Westcott Shore with dimension,
leafy and layered as a swatch of autumn.
In an effort to locate myself in the plum detail
I sat up over the slumbering child
marking the Nippon perfection.

We two rested then in the cushioned earth
in dream becoming one with the dwarfed trees
stilled in their horizontal stretch over gulls on the strand,
the Pinnacle rising in the mist,
umbrella upon umbrella of shelter.

I tended my child throughout the first salutes
of finch, the breaking of water by perch
leaping for mayflies.
We yawned and moved slowly then,
our feet kicking the fabric balloons of gear.
In unseasonable heat, we collected our bearings
watching our center swirl,
spun off the pinwheeling crests.

BRINGING LIGHTS

"Every day half a darkness."
— Artie Gold

Exchanging the oversize lights
for the right Christmas bulb size; the one task
that needs doing. Remember how you felt
humility? Father watched the leaf fire,
kept the leaves in bounds. Your heart
skips. You watch the nova in the sky;
fall away with it; wake from the dream of fire lions
screaming. The cartographer stoops for cigarette butts.
Suddenly, the mix lights: this wanting to burn
with sustainable heat, from smoke to warmth
with an inner light.

Matches may be dangerous. Once children
struck phosphorous, and burned the curtains up.
The subway rails flick off sparks. Your hands
open like an oriental saint's; you imagine your hands
lit with a beam you want to bring to your mouth.

The smoke filled cabin in Stowe
because the damper is stuck
or the fittings wouldn't mesh. Friction
under tension. The smooth slide of brakes,
engines cooling in the Boston evening
while snow twirls around the street lamps,
reminding you of kindling taken for campsite
in winter. A bonfire at Newport Beach.
What you would do with them. Snapping
forbidden. You arch into the cave
a shadow.

If you are patient, Mother said (but not too often —
it was her secret not to talk of fire)
you will learn to swim. She loved the way
you stroked the deep blue water. Your child won't bathe
even if grandpa knows
so you try to avoid this device. Strong emotions
knotting intentions.

Beliefs like Christmas, remember? Irrational meant
a stubborn refusal to think, not
the opposite of what is plain to the eyes.
You strung those wires hours before the decoration
could be hung. The dark train runs into Fenway Station.
The curtains rustle. Pouring in libations for the tree,
resolving in the New Year not to smoke,
you find your hands on your lips.
Reflecting on the trip to the store, for at least that moment,
you know you will go: an act of faith
exchanging the oversize   lights.

CATCH

I take one day from the year to drift
among the cold and sea-like state that birthdays
were for you. Treasures like the rubber
boat went off fast, lost brilliantly
in spring's first river rafting spree. I fall
into the water to see what I've missed.
Fingers cannot find you. Birthdays. What
I wished to mark. Chart gone. My own hands
braced to arms, hooked and clawed, swim
about the wreck till air begins to burst. I see
gardens, opals, coral, the light turned gold
and breathing wholly out, alone, spiriting
to surface brings me face to face with you.
Just Pol believes me when I get on board.

SONNET IN YELLOW

                My unmarried friend
tells me how her daughter will be pleased
to get Stretch Armstrong for a birthday gift.
I put the *Newsweek* up and hurry off
to take our Sendak book she doesn't want
to swap for Ionesco's Story No. 4.
Leaning on the clutch I catch myself,
the stop light red at noon: I see Max threatening
from the cover, cake fork poised, another Rumpus—
I give my boy Josette, her Daddy and
their clever games while Adam brings to Brook
a rubber man to pull apart.

Hot
Teas

Twig Tea

Well after Montreal's International Fireworks,
the day before a usually blistering
American Fourth, this summer's infected
by Chernobyl and the venting
of Mighty Oak in Nevada,
is cold as mid-October in northern provinces,

and the beach towel I've draped
over rain-soaked cushions
grows clammy, clings when I sit,
drives me like a squirrel
inside to collect sticks:

I draw a cup of kukicha tea,
mellowed three years before it is cut,
through the changing seasons,
richly oxidized
in its maturity. Is age or conditioning
a first clue? But so hot! Oh, is that hot!

I burn my tongue in the telling of it.

HAIKU

"You become dented. Your priorities change. Some people
can see it and walk by, saying it's terrible. I can't see it and
walk by. Too many people walk by."

—Naomi Bronstein, activist with Heal the Children, upon
being asked why bear the expense of bringing children
with congenital heart disease to Montreal

Bronstein kisses Chong Chan,
handling his heart in August:
dear Valentines.

A DINNER PARTY

(for Hannah Bond)

What? She was saying.
Outside, later, by the garden
she found a lawn chair.
No one raised a voice
until she came back inside.
Was that all she needed?
The lawn was so green in those days
it grew as wisdom does
in seconds. We have no true measurements—
a cup, a tablespoon, a table—
for the shape of our waiting.
What we hoped would be inviting
in our preparations—
the meatloaf, baked potato, salad—
she came back and took
iced tea, first
like a tuning fork.
Though neither of us knew
a response for tea
we both joined in to listen
before she spoke of needs.

CALL THE DOCTOR!

(for Naomi Bronstein)

"But exactly what," she may be saying just this minute,
"were they doing with their time and their tables,
like the Norton Simon painting of Snyder's
Still Life with Fruit and Vegetables, spilling
earth's wealth — split squash, roots and cabbages,
eggplant and apricots, walnuts, figs, cranberries,
and thirty pounds, at least, of grapes
into a 1¢ existence?"
                              Her hair tied back
on the sixteenth day of her fast,
                              she may stand close to the plastic bin
filling with odd bills, arctic loonish,
moving smoothly in her space, maybe
                    the last of her species

                    but those eyes
                                   count on the children
                    with perfect sense
              of hearts' disease
                              where artichoke and kale
              sound like Greek to the dying.

THE TEA CART

It stands, holds up service:
if exceptionally neat and versatile,
it's yet an object,
designed to be
easy and attractive
post-buffet:

it's set
with respect for very limited content—
dessert and coffee, whipped cream—

misnamed vehicle

and soon empty.

How To Steep

We have so much time on our hands,
            five minutes,
                  or a few minutes,
or three to five minutes, depending
            on your authority,
to ensure uniform strength.

Alone and together, there's just so much time
to renew decisions, change directions,
pour chaque verre
to kettle a new brew, and quickly.
Tea steeped too long
becomes cloudy

like the day you wonder if you should wash the windows.

HEART PATIENT

"Congratulations. Quebec cabinet approved
Canadian daily rate for children coming
to Montreal. Love Herb"

—telegram to Naomi Bronstein, *Montreal Gazette*

In her absence
he pictures her
in Seoul,
washes the dishes,
calls his mom.

Where she is,
she labours for children,
adopting as daughters and sons
and taking information,
making connections,

and smiling as youth
disengages before her eyes.
This is hard for him
and she knows it, as he knows,
and loves that love waiting, working with him.

MEAN MECHANIC

I feel as though I've jammed a brake
into the wheels of life, committing a sweeping portion
of life's honey, time, to scholarship, with a certainty
of disengagement, not damage, a psychic *coitus
interruptus*, scrubwoman of life later
practicing rhythm when it counts. My act
is no rebellion but a further response akin
to interference with closing elevators into which
I've thrust my briefcase or glove
to drive the door open,
if not on my own behalf, refraining from embarking,
then for some one other. I pour upon the ear
the six partitas of Bach, recapture
the image of a child I shook by her feet
to recover the jackball she swallowed
the day her mother took off for the races,
and the sinking swimmer when I was nine
who couldn't have made the edge
had I not come along underwater
to midge her up, repeatedly. I edit my memoir :
it isn't a matter of liking my work —
today I barely get to it— riveting steel girders
for the mind, — but an instinct,
like the gibbon's who mates for life.

ANOTHER TRY

You go for it—the water is too fast—
You see it make a shaft of muddy planks
that curl like potato chips, that regular,
geography and physics might
as well be a press,
the mechanics of the river bed
so affect the flow. But the simulated boards,
a lattice of puncheons, parquetry
that it then shaves, the peeling streams
also toss off notions:
your life is this same river,
and you don't even know it.

You make and break uniformities
by the thousands
for your own kinds of reasons.
Sometimes there's little light
and you list and turn, in sleep, awake,
not sure, usually, where you are.
You go in your tracks,
disturbing the bottoms and edges,
turn stone towards stone
and lift a simple million bubbles.
What you motion travels fast,
steers off; it's hard to imagine
what you thought was less.

GOSSIP

Hot tea, perfect, it says in the index.
So I read on finding that black tea, green tea, oolong
and exotic perfumed teas may come from the same plant
and that cloudy iced tea sparkles again
with reheating without boiling.
Teas hot, spiced or iced, all require five minutes
of covered steeping: from *Better Homes* to *Betty Crocker*
I turn for information about do-ahead tea and table settings
while discovering how a tea merchant stumbled on tea bags
by distributing samples in silk. "Ah,
the humble tea bag," I can just hear my son sighing,
as if a child could understand the simple elegance
of a tea gracing the end of the table
farthest from the door
after a divorce.

BRAVE PERSON OF THE FOLDED PRESENT
(ALMOST LEFT OUT OF THE BOOK)

She steps with difficulty down the stairs at Peel
— loafers to steady the arches,
unburden the spine — behind a hari krishna nun
who moves, unnoticing, into the tunnel;

slowly she moves to the tête
past post-leaning observers,
her black hair sleek to the uneven shoulder,
gently swirling, as arms balance the rigid stride,
rather smoothly courageous
and classy
in her calm.

EXPLANATION

". . .that this may be a sign among
you that when your children ask
their fathers in time to come, saying,
What *mean* ye by these stones?"

Joshua 4:6

Upthrust through the gneiss layer
by great pressure and heat,
cooled, cracked, and crystallized
and eroded away,
the Odd Man left rock and frog eye
behind the Joshua tree:
the salt shaker for the dwarf
by the rumbling wine cask solidified
and the thinnest berry paled
and dried for the serpent's toy.

Out there, the wind cooed too noisily,
and it was snuffed. The chaparral herded the jackrabbit
so fast the air grew dry from the friction,
sent summer midday temperatures four feet above the ground
to 125
a foot above to 150
an inch above the 165
on the surface to 180
till the lily could sing: "Look for life! Look for life!"
in the place that was given it
drilling itself upward for oil
where it found rain
and invented the rattler
in its discarded tongue.

PESOS IN A FOLDED PAPER

Someone else will have to write the poem about Honduras
where row upon row of seated soldiers
exercise under my sun,
our sun, on this hot planet

as if they'd parachute up from earth
like fingered cactus ready for departure in a vacuum
by means of the "fifth force," a wind,
my wind, your wind, in this one world

at the same moment I want my words spoken, published
without a hitch, for once dazzling like a star
off coyote's blanket, ready to go someplace for change
like sugar cubes in a cup, my sweet,
our sweet, in this curve of late October.

Against this extraordinary backdrop,
two children of divorce, refugees
of more northern misunderstandings,
refuse in unison to sweep the leaves in the yard

and their fight, my fight, our fight is not
against this Air Force firefighter, calling "Oh, Yolaanda,"
trekking to a brothel where a woman's poised, —

apparently he has her — a sister, our sister,
for better reason keeps us
till we all break free from Limbo.

TEA AND SLUGS

"... the life of the individual has meaning
only in the service of enhancing and ennobling
the life of every human thing."   —A. Einstein

Outdoors under Chinese lanterns
a lad of seven approaches my adult friend
urging her to try
the *soup de jour*
with Indian spices, incessantly

while I'm thinking eagerly
to have my friend's attention
unbothered by the illkempt, unbathed,
intrusive fellow
who barges in anyway.

Surprisingly, she knows the boy,
repeats his name,
answers his multiple questions as other
unwashed youngsters approach
and the single mother disappears from their table
before we resume our talk.

The youngsters shake an overhead branch,
releasing debris. The same little boy brings
from the decorative fishpond two slugs, places them
on the table beside my childless, patient friend
who looks up, unruffled,
from lemon mist tea,
muselike and kindly, saying firmly as a parent,

"Put them back in the fishpond, Justin,
where they can live," checking the piracy
of snail's karma and ours
by what is unfinished among strangers.

THE EXPECTANT UNEXPECTANT "MOTHER"

Never the less. Remember this. She lives
with and through, as in through time,
not through substitutes, in intervals,
thoroughly lovingly. That is, she *especially*,
in her flesh and blood potential, resting, working,
brings ingredients to mind: the digital watch
in a thimble for yesterday's torn dreaming—
in the revolving door of her fertility
she tries to keep her lunch from being crushed
while someone pushes her. Her phone off,
she takes no messages. Her bed newly raised from the floor,
she labours with dignity, tall taskmaster, or
over her cane, smiles at the young driver,
who offers a car. Is she calling? Sleeping?
Dreaming half-awake? If she isn't grooming at a mirror,
she could be, for her darling. Who could know?
Why couldn't she have one? Or children! Why couldn't she?
Have several? Adopt them, all she really needs, really,
or not, exactly as she makes it, or cannot,
in couples, groups, whatever,
but never the less
and not without appointments,
customs, pastel self-extensions.

Kill Devil.
Hills

SOUTHERN TRIP PROMISED IN DREAM

Soft little Kitty Hawk
eyes of a seal point Siamese
bright blue as jewels, round
and slanted, making slow conversation
        Susan Sontag is a genius
        she purrs and tells
lies down on the bed
her spine arched and light as a hay stack
        flying in
like a Boeing 707 her other part
        a white-wing-gray-striped
                musical encore,
                her somnolent tune
high and whining, erratic.

DETAILS OF A PRELIMINARY LONGING

From slow, deep conduits
plans rise up;
I correct my little map,
through Harrisburg near Middletown, decide:
detour. I will clip to the coast.
Begrudging the bypass,
conducted on the Garden State Expressway,
in Perth Amboy I will sleep at campground.
How I long to take in everything!
What late plans I make,
pushing my drowsy body into the night hours
under the lamp
for there is going to be less gas, you know;
there is going to be less gas
and I tack my way down quickly:
to Philly, Baltimore, D.C., Richmond, Raleigh.
I would dally all along the route,
see the zoos and museums, great statues
and Atlantic City, walk the shores of riverbeds
too swift to plummet
and wide!

Kitty Hawk and the Atomic Sub

April 7, 1979

Forty-eight hours to D-day
departure at half-past two
all signals set for countdown
the house clean, the cat
who will bear kittens while I'm away—
her name, East-er, probably on Easter—
content with the closet I've readied
and this was how Amelia Earhart
might have prepared two days ahead
for the long night solo
in her rickety ship. The engine tuned,
my one dread is located center of seaboard:
tonight I listen again.
Eight days since the accident,
a Trident sub is launched,
and things are still ticking in Harrisburg.

LATER BY MINUTES

It would be nice to make this a love letter
since everyone can read it
but how do we say "love" with the same breath
we say "warning"? How
navigate the shores against the eerie
sizzling glow of the unknown?
If I make this a love letter
and each embrace
fastens us into lies
we lose everything. I stand
this far away from you:
the distance of the flat glass screen
from your lead-protected heart.

AGAIN, ON APRIL 7, 1979

Granted, as a child I was said to be a dowser.
I do not know what special power
pilots like Wilbur and Amelia had;
this is a speechless gift
to carry a willow branch
to a source of flood-tide underground.
Alison told me it may be tonight
with her lambs. My cat is ready, too.
The atomic sub pushed off from shore today
in the colourless depths
bleeping its Morse messages.
Over and over, the water.

MEDITATION ON GARDEN STATE THRUWAY

Sleeping to the sound of vaulted steel
and rubber roaring with an arctic wind
I see morning differently from this rest stop
where the scarcely melting snow
still releases a minor waterfall
through restaurant glass; washed up,
the drudge-clouds snap loose;
a pair of geese wing south over the high-power lines
instinctively with the Interstate
touched and affected by machine and fumes;
to them the roadway's
longer than the Amazon
wider than the Hudson
only rarely a monstrosity.

SLEUTH

Nearing the Delaware River, I spy
an apple tree shook out in blossom
and right then a blue heron rises—
first I've ever seen—
oblique bill and skull and wing.

Even in the rush to locate a rest stop
and refuel, this forbidden passage
into spring
makes me a time traveler.

Here in Delaware, less than a mile
from Maryland and its belligerent wards—
Bethesda and the Aberdeen Proving Grounds—
spring is launched. Unlike those in the north,
these people seem not to know of Harrisburg.

Advancing along the restaurant tar, I pass
dogwood in full flower, and ask the waitress,
"How far is it to Harrisburg?" to see if she knows
and she says, incredulously, "Harrisburg?
Oh, that's a long way. Seems like
you almost can't get there from here."

I am baffled by her admission.

FIRST HARBOR

The *Howard G. Vesper* pulls through the Perth Amboy;
I watch the tugging of clouds south —
tides west —
as the Chevron ship under US flag
heads north, spinning its radar bar.

Wondering if atomic subs cruised these swift waters,
or if men knew, from my car I ask a fisherman
coming off the wharf.
"Catch anything?" and "What
do you usually catch?"
Then, brinking more difficult matters,
I surge ahead, "What is an amboy?"
Says one old guy, "I think it was someone's name.
Lord Amboy, or something," he says.

In these delicate matters, it seems
one cannot behave too carefully
and yet —

THE AMBOY POEM

This is the last thing to do for the book, the only
page out of order, sequentially, in the final hour
but essential: an *amboy*
is not a man
it is not a mushroom
it is not, after the Greek root, *ambros*
a thing divided
nor a lectern
one can enter either way.
It was settled in the 17th century
and was the capital colony of East Jersey
the name derived from the Perth,
Scottish settlers who were dissenters
Ambo or Ambo Point
taken from OMPOGE, an Indian word for a large level
piece of land
and *anybody* can verify this.

THE ACCIDENT

At Roanoke near Pamlico Sound,
I am travelling the Abermarle Trail
off Cape Hatteras; the connection in the dark
and the gathering fog of coast, the swamp stench,
gives focus to the mission:
to find a place to sleep safely for the night
in this lost world of headlights —

I swerve, but slaughter a three pound frog —

the heavy thump on the wheels
followed by gestures. Grieving.

oh frog. oh froggy froggy froggy!

Just beyond here at Manteo
Fessenden sent messages on the wireless.
Exact center of experiment and time:
Sir Walter Raleigh, his colony, 1585;
Fessenden and the telegraph, 1902;
and just south of here on the Outer Banks
Ocracoke Island where Blackbeard was killed
at Teach's Hole, 1718. We span

five centuries in these parts

ship wreck and bird sanctuary proving
the return of the species, the fog
never changing
nor the scent of swamp.

GEORGIA O'KEEFE'S CLOUDS

Oh, Georgia,
you painted this picture so large
it is childlike
a first memory in clarity
uniform, discreet
quantums of pink-edged perfection
each framed by air
that circulates the blue
the artist, in observing order,
energetic,
undefiled,
in a state of grace, noisy,
showing these
uninterrupted
silent repetitions.

ARRIVAL OF DAY

Readout: have arrived Kill Devil
Hills, Kitty Hawk Monument National Park
Parking Lot, flag pole, power transformer,
suspended water tower, granite obelisk,
telephone poles, nearly a dozen campers and trailers
under the cloud trough level at the Visitor's Center
the day before Easter. Correction. Saturday
to a church goer who hasn't crossed
that runway for some years.

No sense seems left in marking what was,
but the wind beats about the place;
the flag pole chain flogs the memory.

So, I think, you have come all this way,
a pilgrim to the rising at Kitty Hawk,

and just then the sun at 10 am tries to breach,
pushing against a cloud enough to stretch it
thin as light behind a balloon
tension keen with nothing to pull away or join through
the bleak sky save errant faith it will prevail.

Warmed thus, I get out to look around.

GLIDERS

The only hill in all these dunes.
Nothing took off but gliders from here.

This won't be any different, I think.

Stooping to recover handfuls of fossil
shale, for the first time tasting
the abundant onion,
I find myself raising the question

whether these purple martins skipping almost
into the air where I turn my face
see everything
or whether to feel the rise and pull of themselves
like kites
is enough.

THE LULL

Out of what there is I make
this experiment. Wilbur —
the bike wheel to the rail pulls
the glider
ancient as the pyramids;
the track —
contrived legacy,
all invention —
putting the parts to use.

Before sleep,
a monument we cannot lose. Wilbur!

CONVERSATION BETWEEN BROTHERS

"Orville? What do you see out there?"

"Wind's right. Still too foggy to go
verticals and horizontals unclear
complicated background — hardly recognizable
historical flight. Machine and aviator, 1895
wing smooth and reticulating propellers.

"Wilbur — ready for passing!"

Sunlit sky accentuating directional lines,
picking out jewellike detail,
straw on the tail skid,
sunset refueling
strato tanker, Strategic Air Command mission
        'The artist can choose a moment in time
        or a vantage point from which to view (her) subject
        that a photographer would find
        almost impossible to duplicate.'
        — Keith Ferris, *The Aviation Art of Keith Ferris.*"

"Wilbur, do you think we can afford
to be so modern? You sound as if you are planning this to lead
somewhere, a whole history . . ."

"Shhh! Orville! Don't be an ass — this thing
is going to fly. Wind up! Adjust
feet to foot pedals. Spine straight. Be proud,
Orville. The wind is coming up
At Kill Devil Hills."

Letters to Home

Dear Father,

Today, we received at our camp the shipment of an erroneous part, seemingly deliberate sabotage of our plans, the huge lead casing impossibly outsized for our glider.

I do not wish to trouble you about our extreme anguish with this set back. It will delay our experiment by several weeks, at least.Orville and I do not feel we can afford to locate the culprit of this attack, but I am disgusted by the added frustration. Do you feel we are right to pursue our work? We seek your wisdom, Sir. We will give this task up completely if you advise it. This is our most devastating hour. We are without much funds, our progress is slow, and now this malicious monkey wrench.

Oh, father, you are so wise,

how are we?

> Frantically,
> Wilbur

Dearest Wil,

    I am counselling you as best I can to quit with your glider and go after the fiend. I know how much your deadline means to you, now with the wind tunnel tests complete and you set up for optimum atmospheric pressure and wind turbulence. I have attempted to reproduce your last tabulations here in the basement and feel you have got your time table right.

    But you must go after this scoundrel! Let nothing deter you from facing the agent of the mysterious lead part that you spoke of. What good will your instrument be so long as the devil stalks?

> Your father in Christ,
> Milton

Daddy,

Why must you use such strong language? We never called the sender of parts who detained us a devil. Surely you know mischief-makers galore among the Brethren. As for Ori and me, we do not have time for pursuing this charlatan. Thank goodness for the invention of the wireless. We have sent messages today for the correct element; in over 1000 glides into 35 mph wind, our record now is 622½ feet in 26 seconds. Both of us feel we need no further direction in the matter of satan. We intend to get this plane in the air a week or two late, true, but at least, up!

As for the devil.

He was always with us, wasn't he?

Your son,
Wilbur

Dear Orville,

I have been trying to communicate with your brother Wilbur for two weeks now as I know your mother would have wished. I assume you have not forgotten your sister in your prayers, either, and our work with the weekly paper. We recall too well how Otto Lilienthal's two-surface glider got out of order and fell with him; you, too, must investigate the source of disturbance of your plans discussed earlier. I can hardly conceive Wilbur's obstreperous insistence on working ahead with the ship while malevolent forces of evil bent on detaining your debut are afoot.

I am writing you to appeal for an investigation, at least, of the chicanery loose in this project.

G' Speed,
Dad

Dearest Father and Pastor,

    You are right, of course. We do know the identity of our spare parts shipper whose misfunction has cost us dearly in time and spirit. It will accomplish nothing to deceive you. It is a clownish oaf who has been abusive of our apppointments; regrettably, we have lost much of our motley store on his account. However, both of us feel we must once again search our souls as to the cause of this trying obstacle.

    What good is a manhunt when the deed is done? The devil has had his day.

Your boy,
Ori

Dear Wilbur and Orville,

    Boys boys please! Look into your hearts again; pray that this villain who has tampered with your work may be apprehended or give himself up before he interferes with the inventive genius of other flyers. I beseech you to quit your labor, to fast and mediate upon this sinister diddler who would hamper the progress of science.

Milt

My Steadfast Brothers,

    You guys better shape up. Pa's getting sick of trying to humble you.

Sis

Father,

Success at last! The 12 horsepower motor weighs only 200 pounds. Orville flew 120 feet in 12 seconds today and asked me to write to you while he barbecues the drumfish. What a celebration!

You mentioned your concern with good works, yet without our plane, we feel we can finish nothing worthwhile that we have started. Anyway, this thing about the odd part has resolved itself on us. Mr. B. Hoof hoped for us to exult in an opportunity to use his modified magneto and water-jacket in our new design. He has been a nuisance and nothing more, for we have the proper spin on the propellers to counteract torque and have said as much to him personally. We regret the intrusion of this jackal into your lives as well as our own.

Devotedly,
Will

Telegram: Well done comma then comma children period
              For to go without apprehension in the gravest
              error period

              The Old Man

111

WHICH WAY YOU ARE GOING TO FALL

Fast as plutonium
you make a dizzying descent
excited
from this distance
cities swirling in lights
air shimmering
the unopened parachute
unworrisome yet
the clouds, like sea algae you emerge from,
white on black, a photo image,
your life so whole you could be pregnant —
free-fall, spread eagle
in the second stage beneath the cloud cover
detecting irradiated steam emissions,
the country burning,
a tizzy of baled hay,
harbours specked with potential tankers,
and suspended,
you reach for the stuck contraption
grabbing the rip cord
like a wash board
then
at the pack
and fear
like an adjusted engine
fans up
wind pressure on flesh
searing
till your face
comes off in your hands
EEEEEeeeeeeeeeeeeeeooooooooooooowwwwwwwwwwwww!
You clutch your groin
your spirit melting
and cry
"Great Heavens!
The wind! The water! The sun!"

MOVING FROM SLEEP

"Through the smiles and the jests and the occasional explosions, there was clearly an unending quest for advantage, opportunity, finding the common ground and the mutual benefit — and then pushing the thing just a little bit farther. This is the primeval life of the swamp at work ... "

Meg Greenfield, *Newsweek*

At three o'clock this morning the plane
is up, has left the ground
silently
drifts
into the dark
off Kill Hills
white wings soaring
aerofoils and fount corrected
the wing curve or camber such
we hover on the sultry summer heat
in unison
(I had almost forgot
your eyes, this lightness of touch
the triumph
of the soft
embrace
)

PEACH BOTTOM
AND THE TRIANGULAR HAT

Driving back on Easter morning
I am not sure of the exact stationing
of crossroads. Peach Bottom
is a place of triangles. Over the dense alders
the hawks skim, wide-winged and watchful.
These are not fruit trees. Here and there an oak,
oddly pruned, jolts thoughts of stunted growth.
I have crossed the river Delaware
and except for the gray-green slate of water
I do not feel unsafe.
The atomic energy plant is invisible
from this bluff;
all Philadelphia prospers.
Still while I suppose a thought of Zion,
a City of Lights, today more appropriate,
it is a black hat and Bermuda
that I call to mind —
a pirate haven —
its myths of disappearance —
dry sand and crackling heat —
without benefit of fruit —

MAY

The white jet tilts in silence
at least forty acres beyond
the Sheraton Inn, the conical nose
swallowed by renovations,
geometric pilings and scaffold
variations of grays and brick
but around that, another dimension
of crisp sky, pale
and expansive.

THE IRIS OPENS

A week ago, I set it in a blue bottle
and today I come home to this
asymmetric lavender plume

The caterpillar yellow crawling on
the single spear released.

I am home with the barn boards and lox,
the rain drumming its songs
at the windows, the roof, and the doors.

The kitten climbs my nylons
while I sip cactus whiskey from a Polish tea cup.

She scales a crooked stack of books,
sniffs cream cheese and mescal, loving the vanguard,
blind to the growing iris.

Eyes shut, she licks her white breast and arm,
and the iris continues as it was —
dismantling.

About the Author

Marcia Rajnus Goldberg, the second of four daughters, attended the Universities of Oregon, Texas, and Vermont before undertaking doctoral studies at McGill. Her paternal grandparents immigrated to New York in 1900 from Prague, farmed in Oregon, and settled in Sacramento. She traces her love of music to this socialist grandfather's violin and accordion playing and to the nine long years of piano lessons she was given by her parents. A swimmer and part-time backpacker, she married a chemist/oncologist in 1964 and with whom she has one son. Following their divorce, she survived as a single mom baking bread, making candles, hosting poetry readings at The Church Street Center in Burlington, Vermont, an unsurpassed learning experience, and teaching in high schools and colleges. She has completed four chapbooks and several unpublished manuscripts and currently teaches English at Vanier College in St. Laurent, Quebec. She has given scores of readings at Véhicule, Magnus, The Word, Double Hook, Buda Books, The Yellow Door, Café Sarajevo, and elsewhere. She does fundraising readings on behalf of refugee relief, environmental and peace mission organizations, and to benefit battered women. She has collaborated with Burton Rubenstein on a series of lyrical films. She shares her Saint Henri flat with seven cats and very often cycles from the Atwater Market along the Lachine canal in Montreal.

About the Cover Artist

Bede Urich is a multi-media artist/designer whose art in acrylics and oils are based on movements ranging from small circles to large ellipses, sometimes interspersed with or layered upon text. Her work is characterized by a play between soft, textual surfaces and strong, solid, structured masses. A polished professional whose imagination and innovation have carried her from Milwaukee and her rigid European ancestry to all parts of the United States. A mother of three sons, her textile and surface-design works can be found in private collections in Milwaukee, Chicago, Minneapolis, Golden, Colorado, Los Angeles, Santa Monica, Carmel, New York, San Francisco, San Diego and Burlington, Vermont. The recipient of a University of Milwaukee grant for computer assisted art, Bede, in a tiny LaJolla studio, created free-form watercolours on rice paper. These exciting combinations of colour, texture, and rhythm are marked by the calculated structure of strong black lines. Her three-dimensional works include innovative boutique apparel, painted furniture, ties, umbrellas and floor coverings. Each is an original painting of design on design, alive with movement, awash with colour, and in harmony with nature.

OTHER EMPYREAL TITLES

POETRY

Experiments in Banal Living, by Michael Andre
Fields of My Blood, by John Asfour
How We Negotiate, by Maxianne Berger
Fire and Brimstone, by Barry Dempster
The Caged Tiger, by Louis Dudek
The Ultimate Garden, by Patricia Renée Ewing
New Poems, by Yuki Hartman
Grounding Sight, by D.G. Jones
Wild Asterisks in Cloud, by D.G. Jones
THE SHADOW TRILOGY
(The Compass; The Mystic Beast and *The Yoni Rocks)*
by Stephen Morrissey
Mythographies (1990), *A Demolition Symphony* (1995).
and *Beautiful Chaos* (1999). by Sonja Skarstedt
EAST COAST TRILOGY
(Nature's Grace, Memory House and *Wading the Trout River)*
by Carolyn Zonailo

FICTION

The Space, by Patrick Borden
Winter, Spring, Summer, Fall, by Robert Sandiford

NON-FICTION

Reality Games, by Louis Dudek
Louis Dudek's 1941 Diary, edited by Aileen Collins
A New World: Essays, by Ken Norris

DRAMA

St. Francis of Esplanade, by S.A. Skarstedt

FANTASY

The Legend of Tarrow Tell, by Geof Isherwood and Ann Tolson

AGMV
MARQUIS
Québec, Canada
1999